Mel Willia

Pi   on

Introduction

Leona Lewis is a real-life Cinderella. Once, she toiled away as a Pizza Hut waitress, clearing away tables while desperately wanting to become a singer. Then she won the third series of the reality TV show *The X Factor* and her wish came true – beyond her wildest dreams. Leona has now officially been acclaimed the 'World's Best Pop Female Artist' – she beat Madonna, Mariah Carey and Rihanna to the title at the World Music Awards in Monaco in November 2008.

You might assume that mega-talented, super-successful, gorgeous-looking Leona is a big-headed, haughty and demanding diva. But far from it. Anyone lucky enough to meet Leona is bowled over by her modesty and charmed by her quiet, common sense manner. So read on to find out what the extraordinarily-talented singing sensation, Leona Lewis, is really like, inside and out.

LEONA FACT FILE

Full name:	Leona Louise Lewis
Birthplace:	Islington, London
Date of birth:	3 April 1985
Star sign:	Aries
Height:	5 foot 7 inches (170 cm)
Eyes:	Green and feline
Hair:	Wildly wavy and a honey shade of brown
Parents:	Aural Josiah 'Joe' Lewis and Maria Lewis
Siblings:	An older brother, Bradley, and a younger brother, Kyle
Home:	Hackney, London

Fast Fact!

Leona's dad, Joe, is Guyanese, of Afro-Caribbean descent. Leona's mum, Maria, grew up in Wales, but has Italian and Irish relations.

Quick Quiz

Q) What music did Leona grow up listening to?

A) Leona loved the old school soul, Motown and R&B music in her dad's record collection, like the singers Minnie Ripperton and Anita Baker. She also couldn't get enough of big Eighties vocalists like Oleta Adams and Mariah Carey. The folk, jazz and blues singing star Eva Cassidy became a firm favourite later on.

5

Stars in her eyes

During Leona's first years at Ambler Primary school, Islington, it soon became apparent to her parents that a normal education alone wasn't going to help their daughter make the most of her natural talents. So at the age of six, Leona started attending the prestigious Sylvia Young Theatre School for lessons in singing, dancing and acting. Staff there remember her as 'a lovely, sweet little girl – but very quiet!'

When Leona was eight, Marie also arranged for Leona to have singing lessons with a top vocal coach, Janet Edwards. Janet usually only worked with adult recording artists and stars of big West End musicals, such as Spice Girl Mel C, Sarah Brightman and Michael Ball. But Janet agreed to coach little Leona because she could tell that her voice was something special. She has said: 'At first I just helped her to have fun, enjoy singing and use her wonderful voice . . . but no amount of tuition could change the fact that she – and her voice – have always been exceptional.'

At the age of nine, Leona went to be a

full-time student at another top London stage school, the Italia Conti Academy of Theatre Arts.

Through contacts at Leona's stage schools, Leona was occasionally sent to audition for small parts in theatre and TV productions. Imagine how excited she must have been when she landed the roles. Leona won a small part in the West End musical *Carousel*; she appeared as an extra in *EastEnders*; she once had a small role in the TV show *2 Point 4 Children*; and she also did some modelling for Marks & Spencer. For her parents, seeing Leona's little successes made everything worthwhile, because the whole family had to make big sacrifices to afford the fees for Leona's training. Leona's mum has said: 'We really struggled as we're not rich, but we did it because it was what Leona wanted. Singing is all she's ever wanted to do and there has never been any other option for her.'

Quick Quiz

Q) Are Leona's brothers in the music business too?

A) Bradley is an editor with MTV, but Kyle is a mechanic. Leona has said: 'My younger brother did go to Sylvia Young Theatre School, but there wasn't a football pitch, so he didn't stay!'

Leona's roots

Leona grew up in Hackney, a part of East London. It's not surprising that Leona is addicted to the TV soap *EastEnders* because the programme's settings, characters and events are very similar to the environment in which she grew up. She has said: 'I was taught to be streetwise. There are certain estates I'd never set foot in and my parents sent both me and my brothers to schools outside the area.'

However, living in Hackney has its good points as well. Many people are mixed race like Leona, so she never felt out of place. At stage school, however, it was very different – she was the only one who wasn't white. She has said: 'Some kids would come up to me and say, "Oh, you're mixed race," making it a big deal when it wasn't.' Leona's family sadly couldn't afford to keep her at Italia Conti, and so she moved to John Loughborough School in Tottenham. There she found she stood out because the majority of the kids were black and she was teased because she didn't wear her hair in braids like they did. Leona once remarked: 'I'd go crying home to Mum and she'd say to me, "You're a beautiful girl and you're a part of me and a part of your dad. You don't have to do anything but carry yourself with pride."'

Fast Fact!

Leona's dad worked as a youth-offenders officer and her mum as a social worker, but they were both musical - Joe was also a part time DJ and Marie had been trained as a ballet teacher.

Determined to follow her dreams

Leona became unhappy at 'normal' school for more than just feeling like an outsider. She found it deeply uncreative – and begged her parents to take her out. Leona was not just desperate to sing, she had begun expressing herself through songwriting too. She wanted to develop talents in every aspect of the music business, including playing instruments and learning recording studio skills.

Fortunately for Leona, she heard about a school for fourteen to nineteen year-olds called the BRIT School – the only performing arts school in Britain that is totally free. Despite it being in Croydon, a long way from her home in Hackney, Leona was determined to attend. The BRIT school has an extremely good reputation and competition for places is extremely stiff. All applicants must have good educational grades, as well as going through a tough workshop and rigorous audition to test their talent as a performer, and an interview to assess their attitude to hard work and their ambitions for the future. Fortunately for Leona, she won a place!

Leona says . . .

'I'm like my mum because she is sensitive and it's easy for us to cry, and I'm like my dad because he's very ambitious.'

Studying For Success

Many people think that winning a place at a prestigious school for kids who want to work in showbiz, like the BRIT school, is like being handed a golden ticket to succes This couldn't be further from the truth. In the Eighties TV series *Fame,* a dance teach at a school like this told her starry-eyed students: 'You want fame? Well fame costs. And right here's where you start paying – in sweat!' For Leona, studying at the BRIT school meant exactly this – she had to put in even more hard work and dedication than for any training she'd had so far. For a start, her journey to school involved two hours of buses, trains and walking – *each way*. She must have been tired before the day even began and fit to drop by the time she reached home in the evening. Leona has said: 'You don't think about that if it's something you want to do – and it was all I wanted to do.'

Secondly, Leona had been at top stage schools before. She was used to being surrounded by highly competitive, extremely talented kids all trying to outdo each other. But now Leona was at the age to stress about her academic studies too – and the BRIT School has an especially strong academic record. For instance, in 2008, 99% of pupils gained five or more A* to C

grades in their GCSEs. All students aged 16 to 18 study for the BTEC National Diploma (equivalent to 3 A-levels) and 85% of them achieved the top grade of Distinction.

The pressure was seriously on for Leona – but she loved every minute of it. The school's creative environment didn't just inspire its pupils to aim for fame, it actively encouraged them to find their own particular strengths and develop these special talents as far as possible. For instance, Leona initially chose to specialise in opera singing, but she later changed direction, focusing on singing jazz and blues. She also took lessons in musical theory as well as learning to play guitar and piano, and worked hard on her songwriting, so she could be taken seriously as an accomplished musician. Leona also learned about the practical side of the music business – everything from recording studio technology to complicated copyright law. Leona was in her element.

Quick Quiz

Q) What grade did Leona get for Music at the BRIT School?

A) A, of course!

Fast Fact!

Among the many music students who have graduated from the BRIT school and rocketed to the top of the charts are the stars Amy Winehouse, Kate Nash, Adele and The Kooks.

Lucky in love

Strangely for someone who loves standing up and singing in front of an audience, Leona has always been a very quiet, shy person. However, according to one of Leona's BRIT school classmates, a singer called Bashy, she stood out because of her looks. Bashy told a newspaper reporter: 'I had such a crush on Leona and so did most of the guys in our year. She was the girl whose name was scrawled on the lockers. She got loads of Valentine's Day cards and everyone was desperate to date her. But we had to stay well away from her as she only had eyes for Lou.'

'Lou' was Lou Al-Chamaa, a boy Leona had known since she was ten, because he lived on the same street as her in Hackney. They finally started going out together when Leona was seventeen – and he remains her first and only boyfriend.

With boyfriend Lou

leona says . . .

[About Lou] 'We've been friends for ages and he makes me laugh so much . . . He's my best friend.'

Glimpsing the limelight

Despite putting 100% effort into everything she did at the BRIT school, Leona never really stood out there musically. After all, it was incredibly hard to make an impact when surrounded by so many extremely talented people – for instance, one of Leona's classmates was the star-to-be, Katie Melua. Most people at the BRIT School just thought of Leona as the shy, pretty kid with the big voice.

There were several occasions outside of stage school, however, when Leona was singled out as an outstanding singing talent. She entered two local talent competitions, including one at the Hackney Empire theatre – and she won them both! Leona's spectacular singing voice also came to the attention of local music producer Marley J Wills when she was fifteen. Together, they recorded several tracks including a version of one of Leona's favourite Minnie Ripperton songs, 'Lovin' You'. Wills has said: 'I think she did it better than the original . . .' Scouts from an American record company heard it and thought it was so promising they invited Leona and Wills to the USA for a meeting. Leona must have been thrilled to think this was her chance at a record deal! However, very disappointingly, in the end interest fizzled out and the promised trip came to nothing.

Leona says . . .

'I'll always go to the Hackney Empire or little talent shows because that's how I came through – that's what kept me going.'

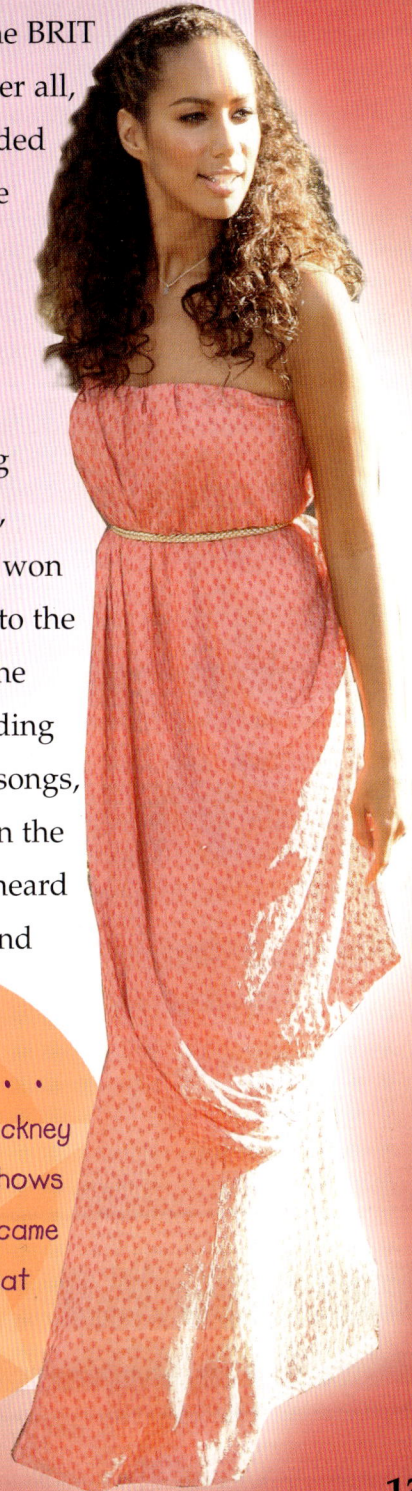

Tough times

Leona is a clever cookie and had her eyes wide open about how incredibly tough it is to make it big in the music business. However, upon leaving the BRIT school when she was seventeen, making any sort of living as a singer proved to be even harder than she had thought. Leona tried everything to get performing work, even drawing on her acting and dancing training to get jobs. She has said: 'I auditioned for plays and shows, and had a lot of setbacks when I didn't get parts.'

Despite suffering one disappointment after another, Leona kept on going. When she was eighteen, her persistence paid off – she won a part to appear in *The Legend of the Lion King* at Disneyland Paris. But fate dealt her a crushing blow. She fell badly while ice skating one day and was left bed-ridden for several weeks and unable to walk properly for months.

Leona had no choice but to give up the role – an opportunity for which she had waited so long and worked so hard. Leona's mother, Marie, once told a reporter: '[Leona] had a six-month contract [for *The Lion King]* and was over the moon about getting the part. When she had her accident and hurt her back she was heartbroken . . . It was a big knock for her, but she was determined it wouldn't put her off.'

Leona says . . .

'I'd always tell people I wanted to sing and they'd say, "Yes, but what do you want to do when you're older?" as though it was an unrealistic ambition.'

Working her way up

Leona realised that if Plan A – auditioning for singing jobs – wasn't working, she'd have to come up with a Plan B. She made up her mind to take other sorts of jobs so that she could save up enough money to record her own album. First, Leona worked as as a waitress in Pizza Hut. Then she was a receptionist in a mortgage broker's, followed by receptionist's work again at a chiropody surgery. Sitting with her telephone headset on answering calls about bunions and ingrowing toenails was a far cry from her dream of wearing a microphone headset and singing her own songs to an adoring crowd of thousands at Wembley Arena!

By drawing on all her willpower and saving hard, in 2004 Leona managed to put aside enough of her wages to buy time in Fulham-based company Spiral Music's recording studio and make an album of her own songs. Called *Twilight,* the album consisted of her eleven favourites out of all the songs she had written since she was twelve. She was thrilled when it came to the attention of scouts for Radio One. Very excitingly, Leona was interviewed on the station by DJ Colin Murray, and she acoustically performed several of the tracks live. However, the CD was not picked up by a record company and so was never released.

The following year, Leona made more demo recordings with a small record label called UEG, but she considered them unfinished and they weren't collected on to a CD.

Leona found herself at an all-time low. For the first time ever, she seriously thought she might have to accept that she would never make it as a singer and that she would have to give up her dream. 'The music thing just wasn't happening for me,' she has remarked when looking back. Leona seemed to have used up every last drop of her fighting spirit, and disheartened, she began to explore the possibility of doing a Sociology degree with the Open University. Then boyfriend Lou suggested for one last-chance shot at making it in music: auditioning for the third series of TV's *The X Factor*. After all, Leona had nothing to lose . . .

Quick Quiz

Q) What's Leona's attitude to waiters and waitresses?

A) She's always polite to waiting staff. She couldn't stand it when people clicked their fingers at her!

Opportunity knocks

By the time Leona auditioned for *The X Factor*, she was twenty-one. Her dad Joe later remarked: 'She was fed up with struggling to make it . . . [She] realised she couldn't keep dreaming for ever'. Twenty-one might seem very young to call it quits on your life-long ambition – but don't forget, Leona had been working hard to follow her dream since she was just five. As she had already more or less made up her mind to give up singing for good, she went along to the first audition without any high hopes. In fact, Leona only really agreed to turn up at all because her boyfriend Lou wanted to have a stab at it himself! Like Leona, Lou had always loved music and singing.

Afterwards, Leona said: 'What people don't realise is that you first get auditioned by panels of producers. It's only after seeing four of them that you get put through to Simon, Louis and Sharon.'

Unfortunately for Lou, the producers' panel thought he looked too much like the winner of the second series of *The X Factor*, Shayne Ward, to take him any further. Leona, however, was put through. 'She was stunned,' her dad Joe said later. 'She never expected it at all. '

Leona with Mum and Dad

A performer with feeling

The song Leona sang for her judges audition was 'Over the Rainbow'. This was the same song that she had sung just months earlier at the funeral of her fourteen-year-old cousin, Billie, who had died of leukaemia. Leona had been very close to her cousin since they were little. While Billie's death was deeply upsetting for her, it also helped to power Leona's positive attitude. 'I've always been driven and seized the moment,' she has said. 'You've always got to take life by the horns.'

Leona could have tried to win the judges' sympathy by turning her personal heartbreak into a drama and explaining her reasons for choosing the song. However, showing typical integrity, she chose not to. If she was going to get through, she wanted it to be for her talent alone.

Of course, all three judges, plus guest judge Paula Abdul, were impressed by her passion-filled performance. Simon said she also looked terrific and Louis agreed, saying that Leona was 'the whole package'. Unbelievably, she found herself through to boot-camp!

Quick Quiz

Q) Leona was one of how many people who auditioned for the third series of The X Factor?

A) 100,000!

Leona with fellow X Factor contestants

The first day of boot-camp was just the beginning of a series of gruelling singing tests, each one more nail-biting than the one before. As always, Leona never looked for the easy option but called on her self-belief and placed her trust in her years of training and hard work. She set herself up for direct comparison with the world's top music divas by choosing to sing some of their best-known, most difficult power ballads. For instance, she belted out 'I Have Nothing' and 'You Light Up My Life' by Whitney Houston and 'Hero' and 'Without You' by Mariah Carey. At last, Leona had to jet off to Miami to sing for a final time in front of Simon Cowell and his popstar aide Sinitta, more than 4,000 miles away from her family and Lou, alongside seven other sixteen-to-twenty-four-year-old contestants – all extremely talented and equally desperate for success. It was undoubtedly Leona's most important audition ever – and it proved to be life-changing. Simon later said that the minute Leona had finished singing and walked away, he turned to Sinitta and said, 'She's in my final four!'

Finalists Ray Quinn and Leona Lewis

A Personal Transformation

Anyone lucky enough to have appeared in an *X Factor* final will tell you that one of the most terrifying aspects of the show is standing in front of the judges to receive their feedback. Fortunately for Leona, Simon Cowell, Louis Walsh and Sharon Osbourne were never in any doubt about her singing ability – they consistently gave her wonderful praise for her fantastic voice and performance and compared her to divas such as Celine Dion. The criticism Leona received was with regard to her confidence and – can you believe it? – her star quality. 'She hasn't got a great personality,' Louis Walsh once said. 'She's very shy and normal.' And the show's vocal coach, Mark Hudson, once commented: 'She just doesn't have that "it".' Bet they're both eating their words now!

However, it's true that at the start, Leona did suffer from crippling shyness and nerves. Series vocal coach Yvie Burnett has commented that to begin with Leona couldn't even look at the camera.

And it's a fact that Leona's uniqueness appeared gradually even to Simon Cowell. He later said: 'It was Rod Stewart who said to me on the second show, "There's one clear star here, and that's Leona Lewis. She is in a different league to everybody else." '

With X Factor presenter Dermot O'Leary

Leona says . . .

'I'm not a loud, extravagant person – I'm never going to be that – and, to be honest, I don't want to be that; I can't fake who I am . . . It was nerve-wracking being judged, having to prove yourself. If I was just doing a gig I wouldn't have been so nervous; I would have just been performing. I've always been slow to settle in different situations, so the butterflies would always come up . . . but it was a good experience because it made me more self-confident.'

A worthy winner

Just days before the *X Factor* final, Leona performed a gig at the local theatre she had such fond memories of, the Hackney Empire. The house was packed and she was overwhelmed by the crowd's reaction. And throughout the televised final itself, presenter Myleene Klass brought live coverage from Leona's East London fans. Leona sang four songs: 'I Will Always Love You', 'A Million Love Songs' (with Take That), 'All By Myself' and 'A Moment Like This' (which was to be the winner's first single). Her rival Ray Quinn was excellent, but Leona was outstanding.

Sharon remarked: 'I know I shouldn't have favourites but . . . it's a travesty if you don't win this contest.' Louis stated: 'I predict you're going to be the next big girl singer from the UK and I think you're going to sell records worldwide . . . You are a world class artist and this time next year, Leona Lewis, everyone is going to know your name.' Obviously the audience agreed – Leona was announced as the winner! 'I think she's one of the best singers we've seen in this country for a long, long time,' declared a beaming Simon Cowell.

Leona says . . .

'It's unbelievable . . . the dream I've been dreaming since I was a little girl has come true.'

Credibility and criticism

Leona's soaring version of the *X Factor* winner's song 'A Moment Like This' was released the week before Christmas 2006. It broke a world record when it was downloaded fifty-thousand times in just thirty minutes and became the biggest downloaded song of the whole year. It became the UK's Christmas number one single, having outsold the rest of the Top Forty singles combined. It stayed at number one for four weeks and went on to sell about 850,000 copies. The resounding triumph of Leona's first single was beyond her wildest dreams and everyone's expectations – however, music industry experts reacted to the news with extreme caution. They were well aware that many previous stars of TV singing competitions had proved unable to sustain initial popularity. For instance, Hear'Say were a group created from the winners of *Popstars* in 2001 who had huge success with their debut single, but split just eighteen months later after their sales slid swiftly downhill.

Steve Brookstein, the winner of the first *X Factor* in 2004 was ditched by his record label after just one album. Leona must have been terrified that her career might head the same way.

A few months after Leona's win, the popstar Jamelia allegedly told an interviewer: 'When Simon stops all this stupid hype about her, that's when we'll see if she can deliver. Like every artist Simon has, she'll fade into obscurity eventually. Leona is a poor man's Mariah Carey . . . [She] may be talented, but she's not worked as hard as me or others in the industry – fact!' (Jamelia has since denied ever making such comments.) Leona was both stunned and hurt at the reported outburst (not least because she had never even met Jamelia) but she chose to rise above it with her usual dignity. 'If people are being horrible to you, it stems from their own insecurities,' she later said. 'Us girls should support each other. I still think she's good and wouldn't say anything bad about her.'

Leona says . . .

'I'm this girl from Hackney who wanted to be a singer but had absolutely no way of making my dreams come true. I knew no one in the music industry, or who to call or what to say. Every attempt I'd made had never got me anywhere . . . People slate shows like The X Factor, but I could never have got a chance without it.'

Quick Quiz

Q) For whom was 'A Moment Like This' previously a hit?

A) Kelly Clarkson – winner of the first season (2002) of *American Idol*.

Time out

Fortunately for Leona, Simon Cowell took good heed of the advice Gary Barlow of Take That had given him during the *X Factor* final. The singer-songwriter had warned the music mogul: 'This girl is probably fifty times better than any other contestant you have ever had, so you have a big responsibility to make the right record with her.' In a move completely opposite to the usual strategy in these cases, Simon Cowell deliberately delayed rushing to get a Leona Lewis first album out. Instead, he swept his new young starlet away from all the media attention in Britain and took her off to the United States to work for a whole year out of the spotlight.

Simon contacted award-winning record producer Clive Davis, the label boss who had launched the careers of Whitney Houston and Alicia Keys, among many other stars. '[Leona] auditioned for me cold and I thought she had a worldwide talent,' Davis later remarked on being asked to work with Leona. 'It was a no-brainer.' Simon approached many top songwriters

Quick Quiz

Q) What was the record deal Leona signed with Clive Davis?

A) It was a contract for five albums for £5 million!

to work with Leona and, as soon as they heard her stunning voice and creative ideas, they jumped at the chance. The quiet girl from Hackney found herself collaborating with songwriters and producers who had worked with world-famous singers including Beyoncé, Madonna, Britney Spears, Gwen Stefani, Rihanna, Whitney Houston and Avril Lavigne. Leona recorded tracks for the album in Miami, Los Angeles, New York City, and Atlanta, as well as London.

Simon and Leona were taking a big risk. By the time the first single from Leona's debut album was ready to be released, it might have been too late to cash in on her *X Factor* success. After all, in the cut-throat music industry new artists emerge all the time. Perhaps the public had fallen out of love with Leona and turned their affections elsewhere?

Leona says . . .

'I knew everyone was saying, "Where's Leona gone? She's just another reality TV show singer who's disappeared," and that some people were writing me off already. But it was necessary to take that time to make the album. We all wanted to get it right. I've always wanted to be a singer and I want longevity in this industry.'

Leona's second single, 'Bleeding Love', was first aired to the UK public on the BBC Radio 1 Chart Show on 16th September 2007, and was then featured as DJ Scott Mills' Record of the Week from 24th September – the day that Leona also performed the track live to hundreds of the British press at a special launch party for the forthcoming album at the Mandarin Oriental Hotel in Knightsbridge, London. One reporter later described the experience like this: 'Some people are crying, and not just her mum . . . The hard-bitten room is won over. A star is born . . .'

Two days after Leona performed the track on the first live show of the fourth series of *The X Factor* (20 October 2007), 'Bleeding Love' was released in the UK and sold 66,000 copies in its first twenty-four hours. It entered the UK Singles Chart at number one and stayed there for seven weeks.

It went on to become the best-selling single of 2007 in the United Kingdom and a major international hit as the best-selling single of 2008, reaching number one in over 34 countries!

On the 7 November 2007, Leona Lewis took up the honour of turning on the Christmas lights in London's famous Oxford Street. Just five days later, her debut album, *Spirit,* was released in the UK. It entered the albums chart at number one and became not just the UK's fastest selling debut album ever, but also the fourth fastest selling album of all time. Britain was mad for Leona Lewis! The album rocketed to the top of the charts in countries all across Europe too.

Leona says . . .

'It was fundamental for the album to be something of substance, something that I could be involved in creatively as an artist, so I could go from The X Factor on to writing songs and just working on myself, developing in every possible way. I am proud of this album and I want everybody else to be proud of the album. People spent money picking up the phone and voting for me; they deserve something great.'

The Darling of America

In February 2008, Leona performed 'Bleeding Love' at the star-studded Brit Awards, where she was nominated for four accolades: British Female Solo Artist, British Breakthrough Act, British Album for *Spirit*, and British Single for 'Bleeding Love'. Incredibly, considering her record-breaking successes, she wasn't announced as the winner of any of them. But Leona was far too busy to dwell on the disappointment. In the 30 November 2007 issue of American magazine *Entertainment Weekly*, Lewis had been named among their '8 to watch in '08' feature and described as 'the next Mariah Carey'. On 17 March 2008, she made her television debut in the United States, singing 'Bleeding Love' on the top programme, *The Oprah Winfrey Show*. While American audiences had previously been put off by the rebellious attitude and appearance of Brits like Amy Winehouse and Lily Allen, they seemed to love Leona's clean, wholesome appeal, as they had done with Dido before her. After several other appearances on primetime shows, such as the *Good Morning America* programme, *The Ellen DeGeneres Show,* and the seventh series of *American Idol,* Leona became the first British female to have a US number one song for twenty years – since Kim Wilde had topped the charts with 'You Keep Me Hanging On'. With their incredible success both at home and abroad, Leona and Simon Cowell had decisively answered all the cynics. Leona couldn't believe what had happened to her – the world was lying at her feet!

Fast Fact!

Experts have said that what raises Leona above other very good singers is her incredible vocal control. However, she insists that even though she has had extensive training, her vocal style is 99% intuition. 'I just sing it how I feel it,' she has said.

A down-to-earth diva

You might well think that Leona's meteoric rise to stardom would have made her big-headed, aloof and demanding, like many of the A-list celebs with whom she now finds herself mingling. Not at all – an interviewer once said, 'She's so sweet and nice it's hard to think of her as a superstar'. Leona doesn't see why, if you're talented, successful and famous, you should be able to get away with being rude and unpleasant and behaving irresponsibly. She never acts like a diva, issuing all sorts of self-important demands and throwing her weight around. She is aware that this means some people in the industry assume she's a pushover – but this isn't the case. 'I never get shouty, but I do speak my mind,' she says. Simon Cowell agrees. 'She is very polite and respectful but she knows what she wants,' he once said. 'She has the confidence to speak her mind.' Also, Leona doesn't drink alcohol, has never done drugs, and would never dream of letting herself down in public. 'I'm not the type of person to come stumbling out of nightclubs. I'll be in trouble with my dad if I get up to anything like that,' she has said. 'I won't do naked, half-naked or underwear shoots. All I want to do is my music.'

Leona is proud of being viewed as a role model. 'There are people out there who think I'm boring,' she once said in an interview. 'But I don't actually see why it's seen as more interesting to take heroin and be completely crazy. . . I'd rather be clean and happy and make something of myself in life. I'd rather be true to myself than sell out and do bad things just to get my name in the gossip magazines.'

Leona says . . .

'I feel and I hope I'm the same girl I've always been and that my situation has changed, but I haven't.'

Leona at home

Despite having a five-million-pound record deal, Leona hasn't chosen to live in a posh part of London or to move to glitzy LA. Instead, she still lives in Hackney, just round the corner from her parents, in a two-bedroom flat that she rents with Lou. Leona has said that she is so grateful to her parents for all they have done in helping her become a singer, that she wants to buy them a house before she buys a place of her own. The only thing Leona has so far splashed much cash on is her first car – a stylish black Mini.

Leona can't understand why people are surprised that she and Lou are still together. 'Why would I dump someone because of this?' she has said. '[Lou's] my best friend . . .' That's not to say that the couple don't argue sometimes. 'Everyone fights,' Leona has said, explaining that they argue about stupid, normal things. She says she normally wins because she's very stubborn and doesn't give in!

The couple are totally committed to each other. 'I think I've found the perfect person,' Leona once commented.

Fast Fact!

Lou asked Leona out for the very first time by sending her a letter in the post – even though she only lived a few doors down – because he was too embarrassed to talk to her!

However, she believes that she's too young to think of marriage and kids yet, and denies that she and Lou are engaged, despite often being seen wearing the same ring on the third finger of her left hand. 'I would like to marry him one day, in a few years,' Leona has said, so – watch this space!

At work and play

Now Leona is an acclaimed worldwide top singing star, her time is no longer her own. She constantly has to jet all over the world for performances, recording sessions, video-filming, business meetings, photo shoots and interviews. 'My passport is crazy,' she says. 'I've got so many air miles, my family is flying free everywhere at the moment!' It's fortunate that Leona doesn't mind working hard. 'I always saw my parents working hard,' she explains, 'and it made me learn that if you work hard, the rewards follow.'

Leona finds some aspects of her work quite daunting. For instance, she was initially quite intimidated by the thought of collaborating with some of the biggest producers and songwriters in the business. 'But I can honestly say that everyone I worked with was really lovely,' she has said. '[My management] made sure I met people before I went into the studio with them, which helped to ease my nerves.' Leona has also had to face the challenge of dancing in music videos. 'Forgive Me' was her first uptempo single and the video entailed a big-budget song-and-dance spectacular – quite a test for someone loves dancing but is primarily a singer. Of course, Leona handled it all brilliantly!

Leona has said: 'I love being in the [recording] studio – it's really important to spend time creating your sound.' But her first love will always be performing live. 'I get really nervous just before I go on stage,' she has admitted. 'When standing behind the curtains, all you can hear is the crowd screaming and it really gets your heart racing. Then when I go on stage, I go into my own world.' Many of the songs Leona sings are big ballads which use all her vocal skills and draw on all her emotions, and they can leave her feeling quite drained. In rare time off, to relax, she likes nothing better than to just hang out with her family and friends. Leona has said, 'I insist on having regular time set aside in my schedule for my family and for Lou.' She likes them to accompany her on her travels, whenever possible. Leona doesn't go to the latest star-filled hangouts – 'You don't want to go where photographers are going to be, not if you want a nice night out,' she explains. She also likes playing the piano and guitar to relax, or watching films or TV – especially *EastEnders* and, yes, *The X Factor*!

Fast Fact!
Leona has a beloved pet rottweiler dog called Rome.

Leona's style

Leona is obviously stunningly good-looking. She electrifies videos, photo-shoots and the red carpet in designer gowns worth tens – sometimes even hundreds – of thousands of pounds. 'I've been able to work with some amazing designers,' she has said. 'It's great to get dressed up and get your hair and make-up done.' Leona favours ladylike prom frocks and Greek-goddess-style maxi-dresses – even though she'd rather have bare feet than wear gorgeous designer shoes, as she is passionate about nature and likes to feel in contact with the earth.

However, when it comes to her own personal style, Leona has very simple tastes. On her days off, she's happiest without make-up, in casual, comfy clothes like jeans and Ugg boots – they have to be fake though, as Leona has been vegetarian since the age of twelve and refuses to wear leather. Leona gets sent a lot of clothes for free by designers, but every time she's sent something leather – such as a gorgeous designer bag or pair of shoes – she sends it back, very politely of course. 'I don't think animals should be killed for our pleasure,' she has explained. Fur is of course another definite no-no. Leona is conscious of other ethical fashion issues, like the conditions of people who work in diamond mines. 'I have nothing bling about me!' she has said. High-street chain Accessorize is her favourite place to buy jewellery. Of course, wherever Leona goes, she is hounded by photographers all the time. 'There's a pressure to look good for everyone . . .

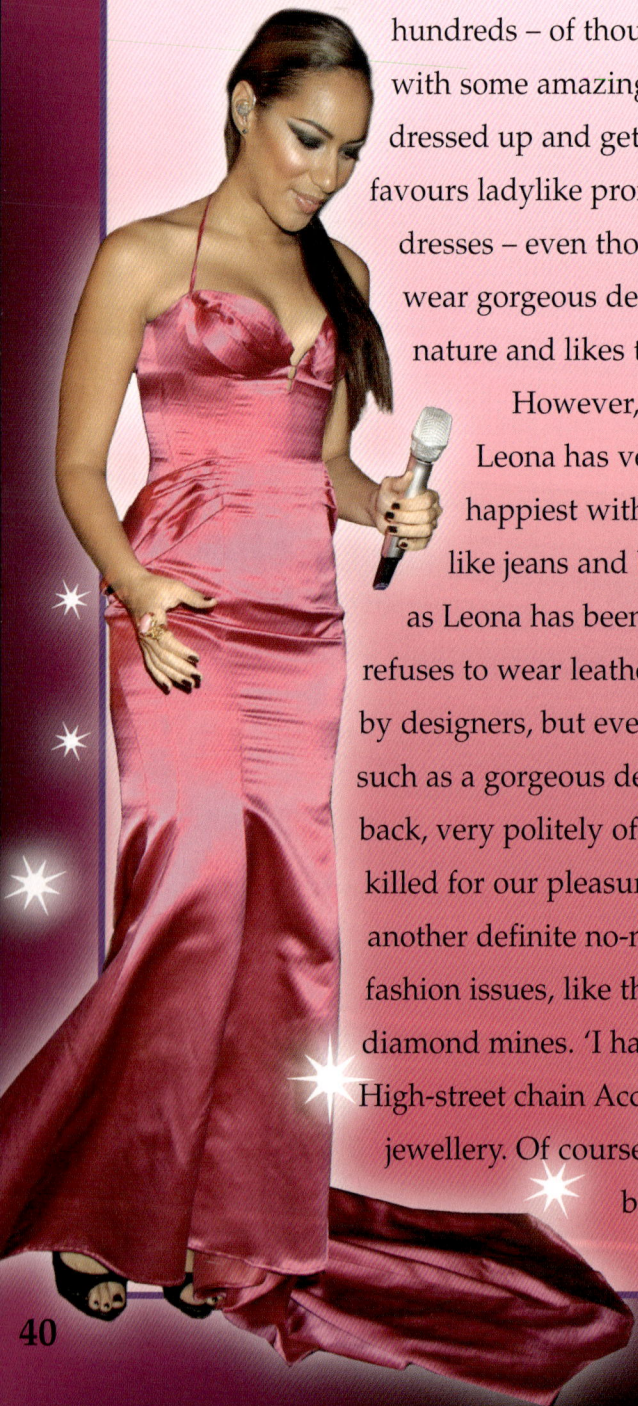

it's because of all those images in the media of stick-thin people,' she has remarked. 'Of course, some days I will feel a bit insecure and wonder do I look all right? But you can't subscribe to these pressures because they're not real. I try to eat healthily. I go riding and to the gym. But I don't think about it as looking good; I think about it as being healthy.'

LEONA'S FAVES

- Favourite album: Hard to choose, but maybe *Thriller*
- Favourite single: One of many favourites is Mariah Carey's 'Can't Let Go'
- Favourite artists: Whitney Houston and Roberta Flack, among many others
- Favourite personal feature: 'My smile – it's kind of geeky.'
- Favourite chocolate bar: Galaxy
- Favourite flavour of yoghurt: Raspberry
- Favourite fruit: Pineapple
- Favourite animal: Dogs

whatever next?

Among all the amazing recording artists from Britain, Leona Lewis is the first *ever* to have a debut album enter America's Billboard Top 200 Chart at number one. She's also the first British female artist in history to score both a US number one single and number one album in the same week.

Leona was honoured to perform at the star-studded concert held in Hyde Park in June 2008 to celebrate the 90th birthday of South African hero Nelson Mandela. She also appeared in August 2008 at the closing ceremony of the Olympics in Beijing, alongside rock-legend Jimmy Page of Led Zeppelin and footballing megastar David Beckham. Her performance was watched by a TV audience of around three billion people worldwide! In November 2008, Leona performed at

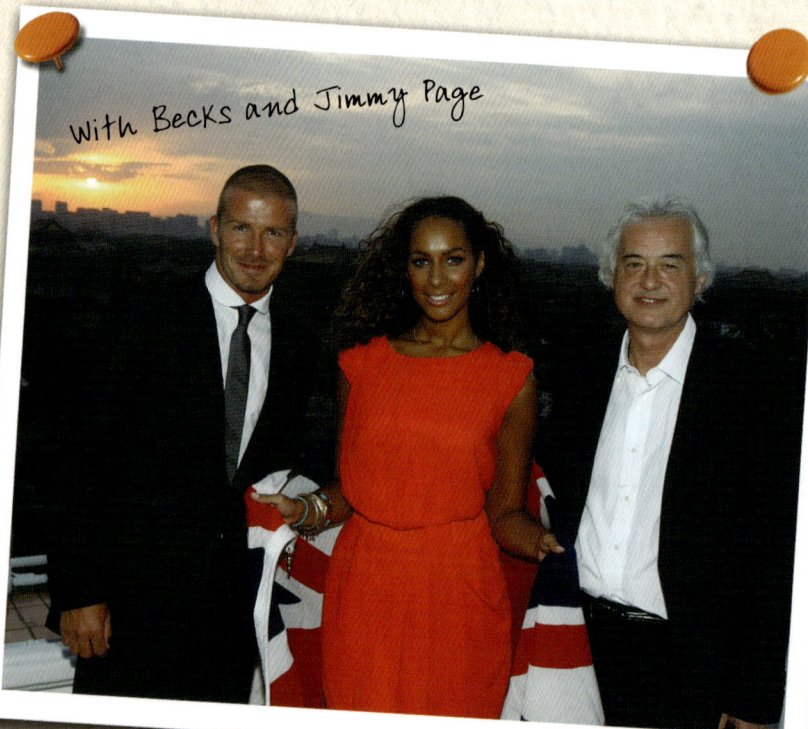

With Becks and Jimmy Page

Olympics closing ceremony

the American Music Awards in LA, and in December she met Prince Charles after performing in front of him at the Royal Variety Show in London.

Leona has been awarded two MOBOs (the 2008 awards for Best Album for *Spirit* and Best Video for 'Bleeding Love'), nominated for three Grammys (Record of the Year for 'Bleeding Love', Best Female Pop Vocal Performance, and Best Pop Vocal Album for *Spirit*), and has won countless other accolades.

Leona has said: 'The music is the main focus at the moment, it's my passion and that's what I like to do.' Leona loves songwriting and plans are underway for a third album and a spectacular world tour. There are rumours that Mariah Carey would like Leona to star in a musical of her life, as she is one of the few singers who can match Mariah's incredible eight-octave range. If this project emerges Leona might well be interested, as she has said: 'I did drama and dance when I was young and I would love to incorporate that somewhere in the future.'

With Nelson Mandela and Annie Lennox

Future ambitions

Leona has many goals in areas other than music. Since becoming famous, she has played a part in many high-profile charity events. She has performed alongside Mariah Carey, Rihanna, Beyoncé and other top singers at a Stand Up To Cancer concert in the USA, has travelled to Africa to raise awareness of the plight of AIDS victims there, she has released a double-A-side single ('Better in Time' and 'Footprints in the Sand') in aid of Sport Relief, and she has become an ambassador for Prince Charles's charity, The Prince's Trust. However, Leona was involved with charity work long before *The X Factor.* As a teenager, she was involved in a project to help kids in deprived areas, and she's keen to support more youth projects.

Leona is passionate about animal causes and is a big supporter of the World Society for the Protection of Animals. She would love to launch her own ethical fashion line, such as a range of non-leather, affordable bags and shoes. First though, watch out for the launch of a sensational 'Leona' perfume.

Finally, there are Leona's personal ambitions. Family is extremely important to her and she would love to get married and have children with Lou one day – when she feels the time is right.

Fergie,
Leona Lewis
& Ciara

Fast Fact!

It has been reported that in October 2008 Leona turned down a million-dollar deal to open the Harrods sale, on the grounds that Harrods is the only department store in the UK which continues to stock clothing made from animal fur.

Onwards and upwards!

Leona is well aware that the ruthless music industry is very fickle and success can be short-lived. She has said: 'I don't take anything for granted . . . This could be my last week.' Surely, however, Leona's got the talent, the looks, the energy and the personality to blaze a trail along whichever exciting future directions she decides to take. Watch out world – this is only the beginning for singing superstar, Leona Lewis!

Quick Quiz

Q) Is Leona scared of anything?

A) The dark and spiders.